WHAT AM I?

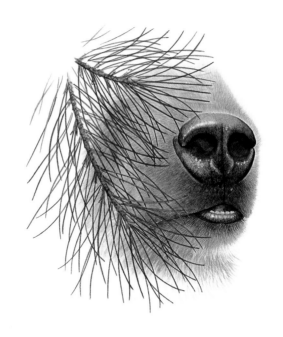

Brown, Fierce, and Furry

WHAT AM I?

By Moira Butterfield
Illustrated by Wayne Ford

RSVP
RAINTREE
STECK-VAUGHN
PUBLISHERS
The Steck-Vaughn Company

Austin, Texas

Published by Raintree Steck-Vaughn Publishers, an imprint of Steck-Vaughn Company

Editors: Jilly MacLeod, Kathy DeVico
Project Manager: Joyce Spicer
Electronic Production: Amy Atkinson
Designer: Helen James
Illustrator: Wayne Ford / Wildlife Art Agency

Library of Congress Cataloging-in-Publication Data

Butterfield, Moira, 1961-
    Brown, fierce, and furry/by Moira Butterfield; illustrated by Wayne Ford.
      p.   cm. — (What am I?)
    Summary: A riddle asking the reader to guess which animal is being described precedes information about different parts of a bear's body, how it behaves, and where it lives.
    ISBN 0-8172-4586-3
    1. Brown bear — Juvenile literature.   [1. Brown bear. 2. Bears.]
    I. Ford, Wayne, ill.   II. Title.   III. Series.
QL737.C27B87   1997
599.74'446 — dc20   96-32111
                                    CIP   AC

Printed in Portugal.
Bound in the United States.
1 2 3 4 5 6 7 8 9 0 LB 99 98 97 96

My fur is soft. My nose is long.
My claws are sharp.
My paws are strong.
Around the forest paths I prowl.
Be careful not to make me growl.

What am I?

Here is my fur.

It is brown and
soft and grows
all over my body.
Can you see my
round, furry ears
sticking up?

The weather is
often cold and
snowy where
I live. My thick
fur coat keeps
me warm.

Here are my teeth.

I use them to eat lots of different things. I like to munch on fat, juicy blackberries.

I like to eat honey, too. Sometimes I follow bees to find their nest full of sweet honey.

Here is my paw.

I have long, sharp
claws to dig up
roots and little
animals from
under the ground.

Sometimes I stand in
the river to catch
food. Can you
see what I am
holding in
my paw?

11

Here is my nose.

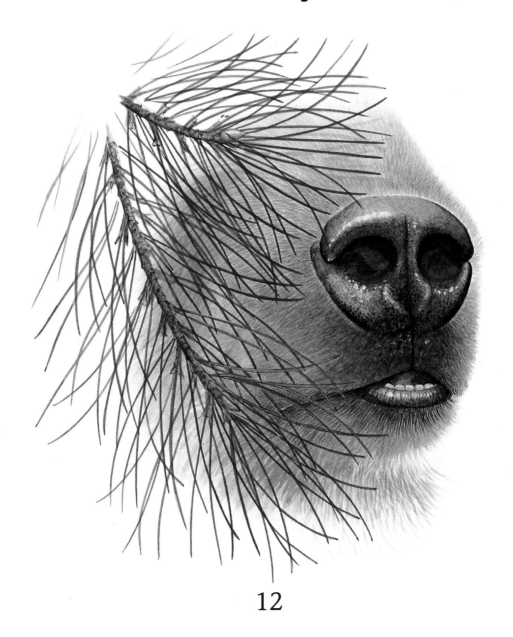

It is called my
snout. I can
smell food from
very far away.
There is no food
at this campsite.

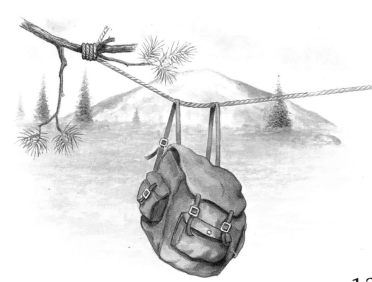

The campers hang
their food in a bag
between two trees.
I can smell the
food, but I cannot
reach it.

Here is my eye.

I cannot see things
that are far away.
Can you see the deer
standing on the hill?
I can't see it, but I
can smell it.

In the winter, I
hide in my home.
I shut my eyes
and sleep for
weeks and weeks,
until it is spring.

Here are my legs.

I stand on my back legs to scratch a tree with my claws. Then I leave my smell on it.

Other animals like me see the scratches and smell the tree. They know I live nearby.

Here is my home.

It is called a den. It may be a cave or
a hole I have dug in the ground.
I sleep safe and sound inside.
If something wakes me, it makes me angry.

I open my mouth and...
growl!
Have you guessed what I am?

I am a bear.

Point to my ...

round ears.

long nose.

furry tail.

brown eyes.

20

strong paws.

sharp claws.

I am called
a brown bear.

Here are my babies.

They are called cubs. When they are born, they are tiny. My cubs stay in the den with me.

When they grow bigger, they go out to play. They chase each other and climb trees.

This is where I live.

I live in the forest.

Can you see a deer, two chipmunks,
a bees' nest, and a woodpecker?

Here is a map of the world.

I live in lots of different countries. Can you see some of the places where I live?

Can you point to the place where you live?

North America

The places where
I live are this color.

Russia

Europe

27

Can you answer these questions about me?

What color is my fur?

Do I like to eat berries?

What else do I like to eat?

Can I smell things that are far away?

Can I see things that are far away?

28

What are my babies
called?

What do I use my
claws for?

What is my home
called?

How do I spend
the winter?

29

Here are words to help you learn about me.

claws The long, sharp nails on my paws. I have five claws on each paw.

den My hidden home in a cave or a hole that I have dug in the ground.

fur My warm, soft coat. It is very thick, and it keeps me warm.

growl The noise I make when I am angry. Can you make a growling noise, too?

munch The way I chew my food.

paws My furry hands and feet. I can catch fish with my paws.

prowl The slow and careful way I move when I am looking for food.

roots The parts of a plant that grow in the ground. I like to dig them up and eat them.

snout My long nose.

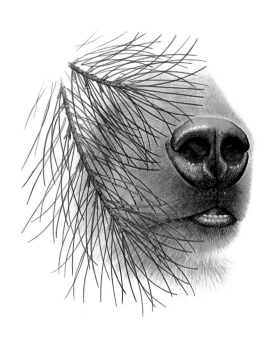